LOVE CATS

A PURRRRRRR FECT... LOVE STORY

BY TONI GOFFE

First published in Great Britain by
Pendulum Gallery Press
56 Ackender Road, Alton, Hants GU34 1JS

© *TONI GOFFE 1994*

LOVE CATS
ISBN 0-948912-30-8

All rights reserved. No part of this publication may be reproduced or transmitted in any form or by any means, electronic or mechanical, including photocopying, recording, or any information storage and retrieval system, or for a source of ideas without permission in writing from the publisher.

PRINTED IN GREAT BRITAIN BY
UNWIN BROTHERS LTD, OLD WOKING, SURREY

GOODBYE

BIG CITY

CITY DIGS

LONELY NIGHTS

DREAMING OF HOME

I MUST NOT TALK TO MYSELF.

ON NOTICING THE OPPOSITE SEX.

FOLLOWING PUSS.

MORE FANTASTIC DREAMS

A MEETING

DITCHED

ANOTHER MEETING

TRAPPED ?

ESCAPE

ALONE AGAIN

A CASUAL MEETING

CAN`T SLEEP

WHAT`S WRONG WITH ME ?

WE MEET AGAIN
HA, HA, HA,

I CAN`T EAT......
BUT SOMETHING`S EATING ME

THIS MUST BE LOVE,
BECAUSE I FEEL SO BAD.

HOW MANY DAYS TO WASH-DAY?

I JUST CAN`T WAIT.

MISSING YOU,
WHO EVER YOU ARE.

I`M PRACTICING
MEETING YOU.

MEETING YOU AGAIN, AGAIN.

THE WALKS

THE TALKS

THE PARTING
(I`LL CALL YOU)

WHY HASN'T SHE CALLED?

HOW COULD SHE BE SO CRUEL?

A FORGOTTEN PUSS
.................DITCHED!

I`LL NEVER TRUST A PUSSY-CAT AGAIN!

THE PHONE CALL !!!!!!!
(IT`S BEEN TWO WHOLE HOURS!)

THE FIRST KISS!

FLOWERS FOR YOU.

BIKE RIDES.

PICNICS.

WEEKENDS AWAY.

PRESENTS !

REALLY IN LOVE.....

THE SIGHTING !

DESPAIR !!

I CAN`T BARE IT !
(HOW COULD SHE !!??)

TREACHERY AND ANGER.....

MURDER ON MY MIND!

HAVE YOU MET MY BROTHER?

GUILT !

MAKING UP.

FORGIVEN!

SLEEPING TOGETHER.

DINNER AT HOME.

TAKEN ILL!

TAKEN AWAY!

WELL, SOON GET!

PREPARING FOR THE FUTURE....

HOME COMING.

HOME SWEET HOME.

DON`T YOU EVER LEAVE ME!

TOGETHER FOREVER ?

WILL YOU MARRY ME?

OTHER BOOKS IN THIS SERIES; BY TONI GOFFE

IS THERE LIFE WITHOUT CATS ? ISBN 0.948912.21.9

IS THERE LIFE WITHOUT DOGS ? ISBN 0.948912.22.7

LIFE`S LESSONS FROM MY DOG. ISBN 0.948912.28.6

LIFE`S LESSONS FROM MY CAT. ISBN 0.948912.27.8